JOHN ADAMS
OPERA CHORUSES
VOLUME 3

CHORUSES FROM THE DEATH OF KLING___R

EDITED BY GRANT GERSHON

HENDON MUSIC
BOOSEY & HAWKES

www.boosey.com

The first time I met John Adams I was playing piano rehearsals for *Nixon in China*. The year was 1990 and I remember vividly both the unbridled joy of discovering his work for the first time and the utter terror that my counting would go awry, and I'd fall into one of those infamous "John Adams holes" where one careens full-bore into a beat of (intended) silence. John was extraordinarily kind to me in those rehearsals and he clearly had a sense of how crazy it is to corral an entire orchestra's worth of activity into 10 fingers! That began a long and treasured friendship, and I have an enduring love, based on those early experiences, of hearing John's operas and oratorios played on the piano.

Over the past 30 years I've played, conducted, and in several cases, premiered John's works with continued joy and (maybe slightly) less terror. As a pianist and conductor with a deep love of choirs I've often wished that there was more music of John's available to choral ensembles. John seems to pour heart and soul into the choruses of his large-scale works and so it has been frustrating that only those choral ensembles lucky enough to be associated with a symphony orchestra or opera company have heretofore had access to this great repertoire. I'm therefore delighted that these newly transcribed versions of some of John's greatest choruses will open up his music to many more choral ensembles and pianists.

I'm hugely grateful to Zizi Mueller for envisioning and championing this undertaking, and to Maggie Heskin for shepherding it through to completion. We recently "test drove" several of these transcriptions in concert with the Los Angeles Master Chorale and I'm deeply indebted for both the brilliant playing and the honest feedback from our four rock star pianists—Gloria Cheng, Lisa Edwards, Bryan Pezzone and Vicki Ray. Most of all I am in awe of Chitose Okashiro for wrestling the unbridled inventiveness of John's orchestral writing into 88 keys, two hands and 10 digits! These transcriptions are imaginative, colorful, and of course fantastically virtuosic. I hope that through them and through this edition John Adams' great choral music will resonate with adventurous choral ensembles far and wide!

—Grant Gershon

CONTENTS

Choruses from *The Death of Klinghoffer*

Chorus Of The Exiled Palestinians --------------------p. 1

Chorus Of The Exiled Jews --------------------------p. 22

Ocean Chorus --p. 33

Night Chorus --p. 41

Hagar And The Angel ---------------------------------p. 54

Desert Chorus--p. 70

Day Chorus --p. 79

CHORUS OF THE EXILED PALESTINIANS
from THE DEATH OF KLINGHOFFER

Libretto by
ALICE GOODMAN

Music by
JOHN ADAMS

Piano reduction by
CHITOSE OKASHIRO

979-0-051-48574-1

Printed 2020

Optional: add tenors from here to m. 108

gradually pick up tempo

(♩ = 94) continue picking up tempo

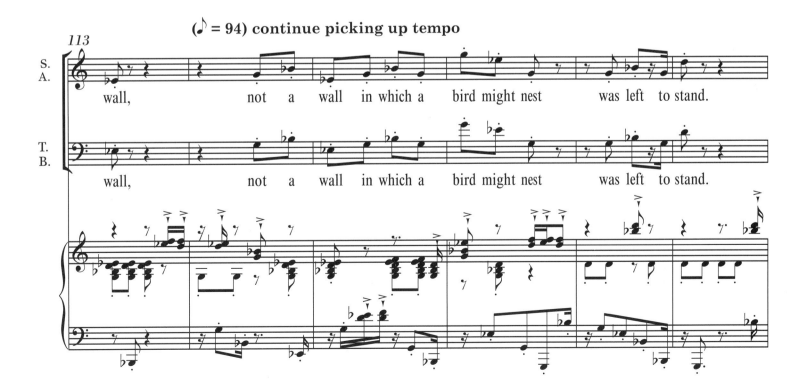

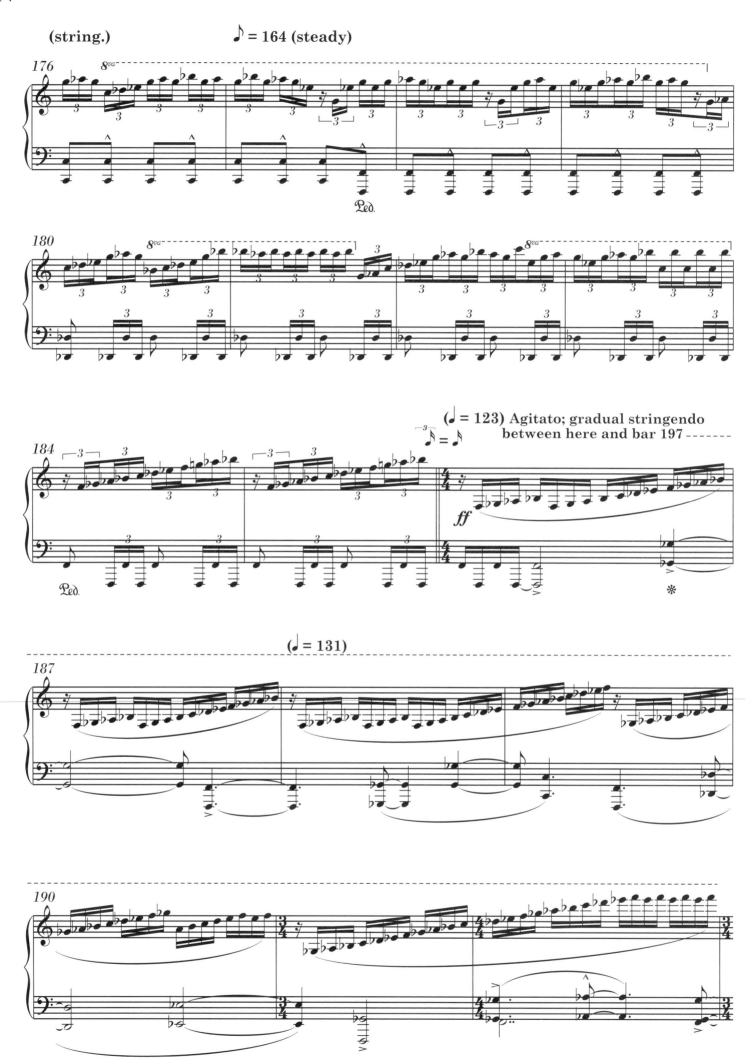

CHORUS OF THE EXILED JEWS
from THE DEATH OF KLINGHOFFER

Libretto by
ALICE GOODMAN
Piano reduction by
CHITOSE OKASHIRO

Music by
JOHN ADAMS

S. pas-sion, which it-self re-mem-bers. My emp-ty hands shall sig-ni-fy this pas-sion, which it-self re-

A. pas-sion, which it-self re-mem-bers. My emp-ty hands shall sig-ni-fy this pas-sion which it-self re-

T. pas-sion, which it-self re-mem-bers. My emp-ty hands shall sig-ni-fy this pas-sion, which it-self re-

B. pas-sion, which it-self re-mem-bers. My emp-ty hands shall sig-ni-fy this pas-sion, which it-self re-

S. mem-bers, which it-self re-mem-bers.

A. mem-bers, which it-self re-mem-bers.

T. mem-bers, which it-self re-mem-bers. O

B. mem-bers, which it-self re-mem-bers.

espressivo

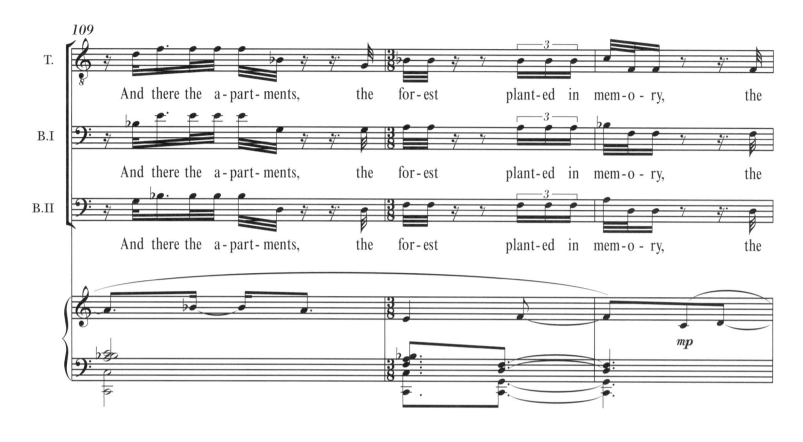

And there the a-part-ments,   the   for-est   plant-ed   in   mem-o - ry,   the

And there the a-part-ments,   the   for-est   plant-ed   in   mem-o - ry,   the

And there the a-part-ments,   the   for-est   plant-ed   in   mem-o - ry,   the

mp

mov-ie hous-es__ pick-et-ed_ by Ha-si - dim,__   the mil-i-tar-y bar- racks,   the

mov-ie hous-es__ pick-et-ed_ by Ha-si - dim,__   the mil-i-tar-y bar- racks,   the

mov-ie hous-es__ pick-et-ed_ by Ha-si - dim,__   the mil-i-tar-y bar- racks,   the

Ocean Chorus
from The Death of Klinghoffer

Libretto by
ALICE GOODMAN

Piano reduction by
CHITOSE OKASHIRO

Music by
JOHN ADAMS

NIGHT CHORUS
from THE DEATH OF KLINGHOFFER

Libretto by
ALICE GOODMAN

Piano reduction by
CHITOSE OKASHIRO

Music by
JOHN ADAMS

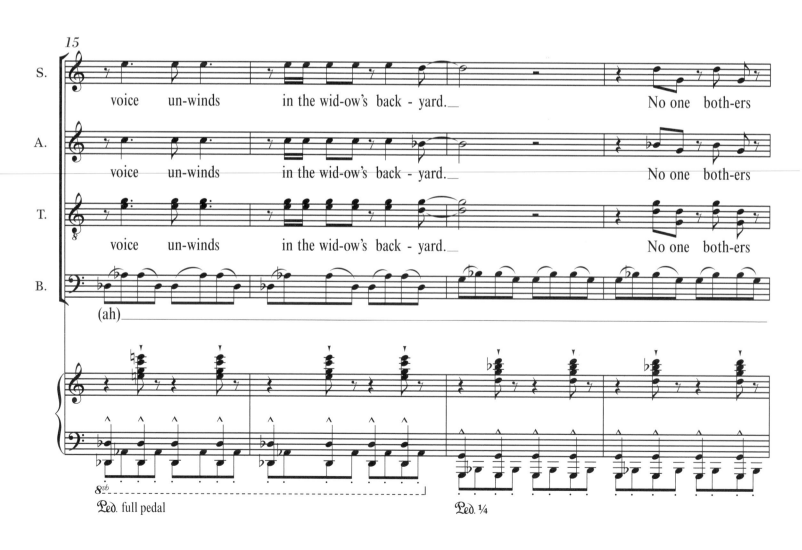

HAGAR AND THE ANGEL
from THE DEATH OF KLINGHOFFER

Libretto by
ALICE GOODMAN

Piano reduction by
CHITOSE OKASHIRO

Music by
JOHN ADAMS

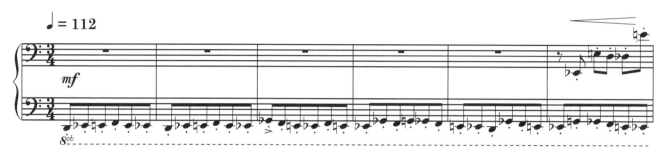

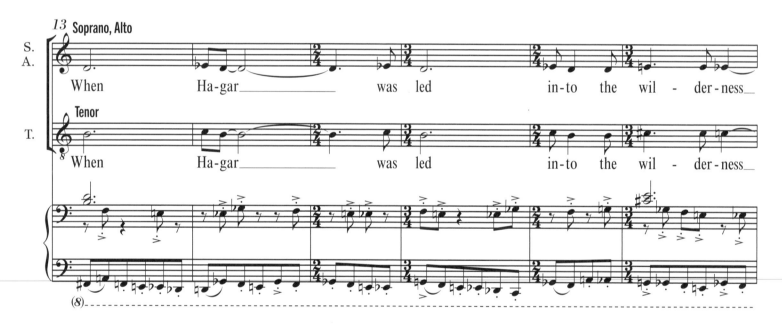

When Ha-gar was led in-to the wil-der-ness

When Ha-gar was led in-to the wil-der-ness

— with some bread and a bot-tle of wat-er and her

— with some bread and a bot-tle of wat-er and her

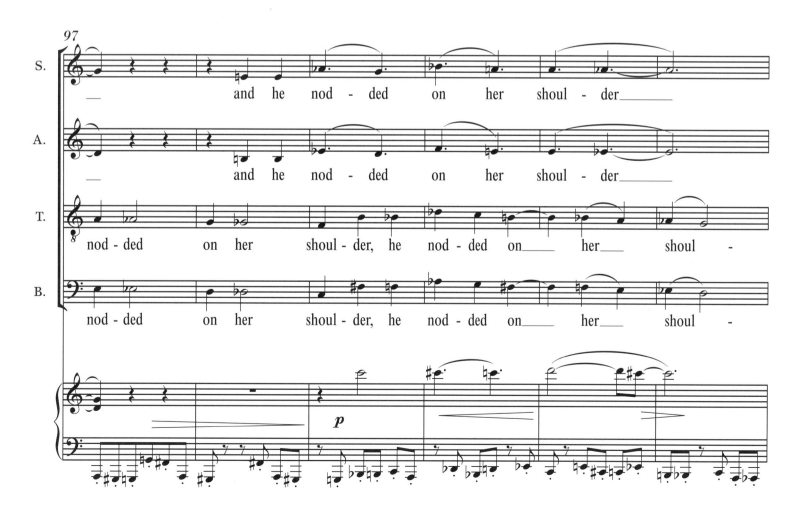

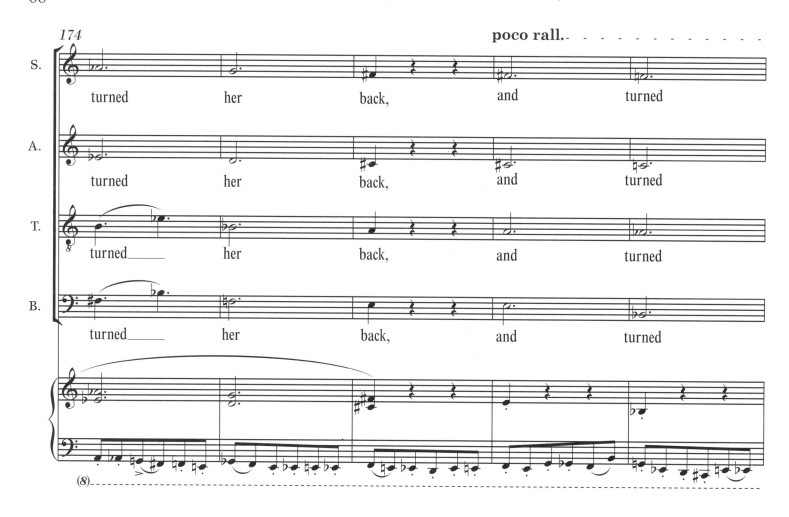

DESERT CHORUS
from THE DEATH OF KLINGHOFFER

Libretto by
ALICE GOODMAN

Piano reduction by
CHITOSE OKASHIRO

Music by
JOHN ADAMS

Female Chorus *(gently, without vibrato)*

Is not their de-sert the gar-den of the Lord?

Is not their de-sert the gar-den of the Lord?

Rain falls_____ on the earth where

and not light - ly on the____ *bi - tu - mi-nous land,____

ob-lit-er-at-ing land - marks;   it

va - nish-es____ be- tween the par-ti-cles_ of rock,   and runs down an-cient a - qui-fers   lined_

* pronounced "bye-too-mi-nous"

DAY CHORUS
from THE DEATH OF KLINGHOFFER

Libretto by
ALICE GOODMAN

Music by
JOHN ADAMS

Piano reduction by
CHITOSE OKASHIRO

* N.B. Altos may double the Tenor line through bar 25

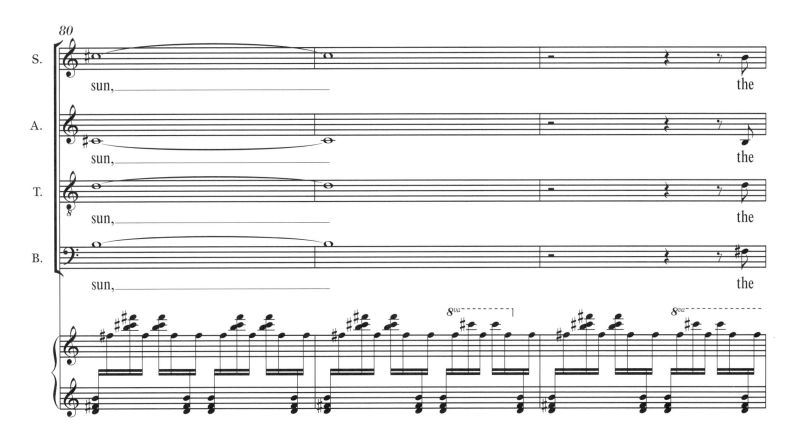

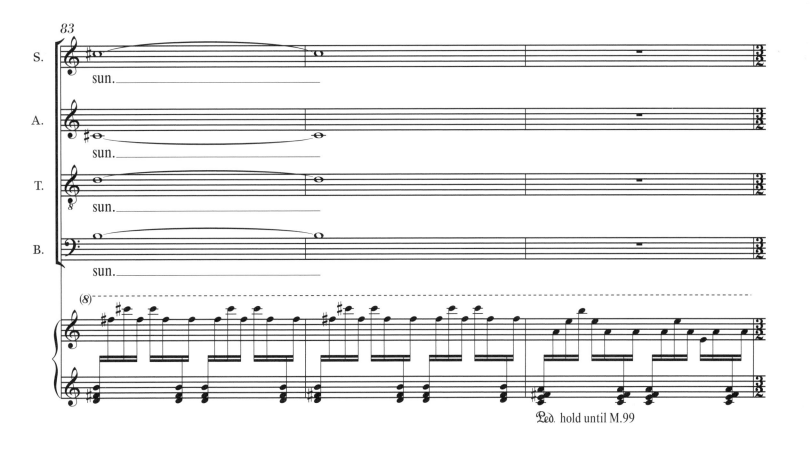

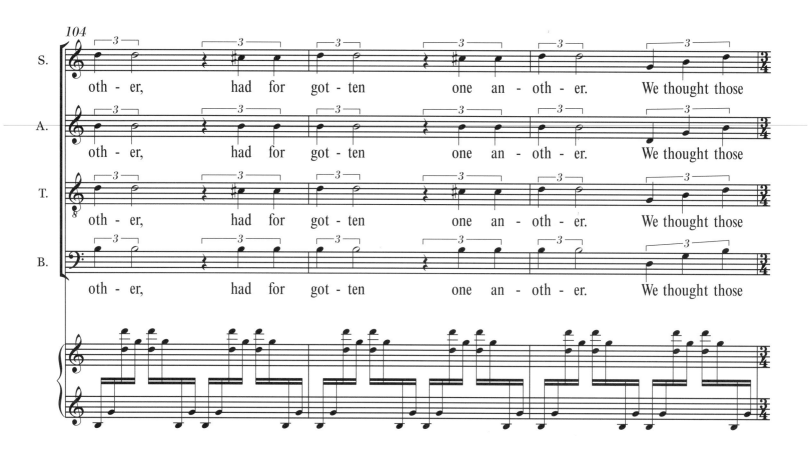

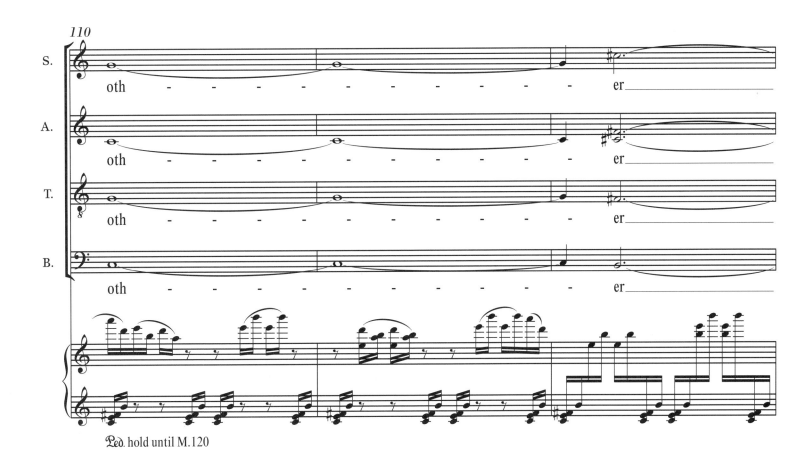

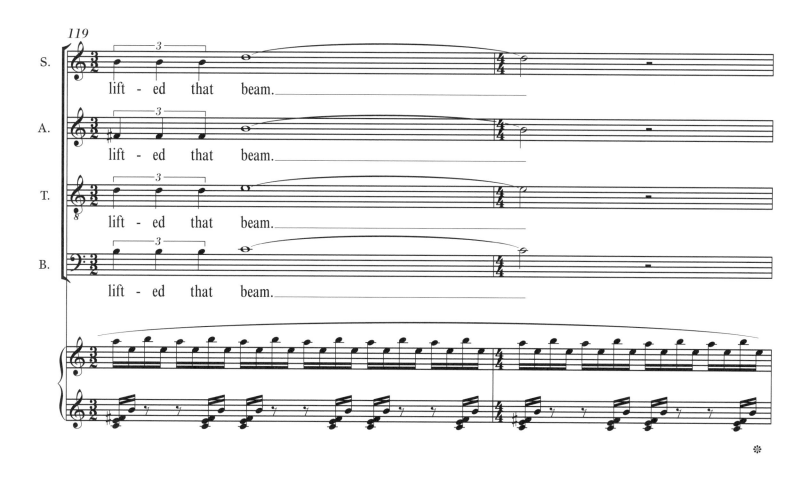

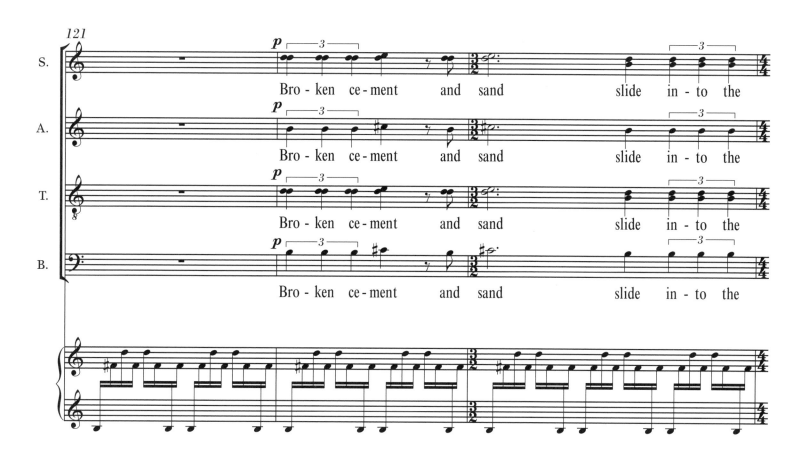

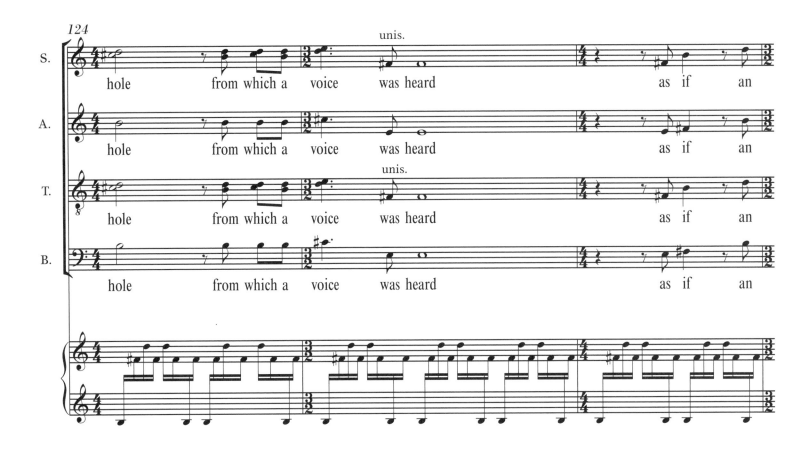

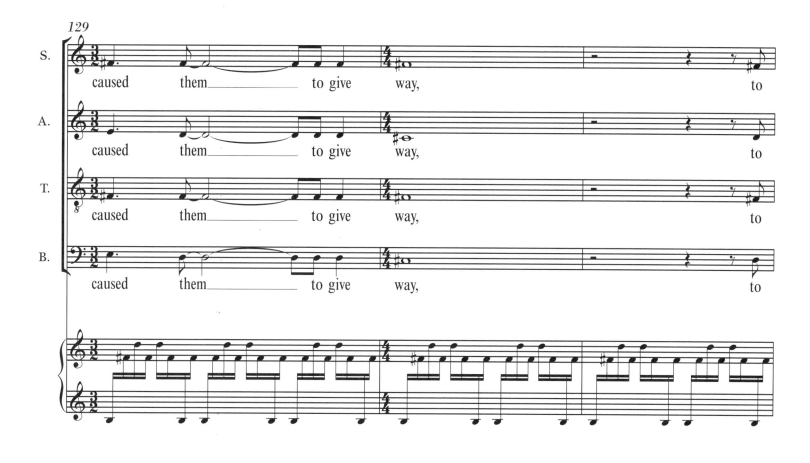

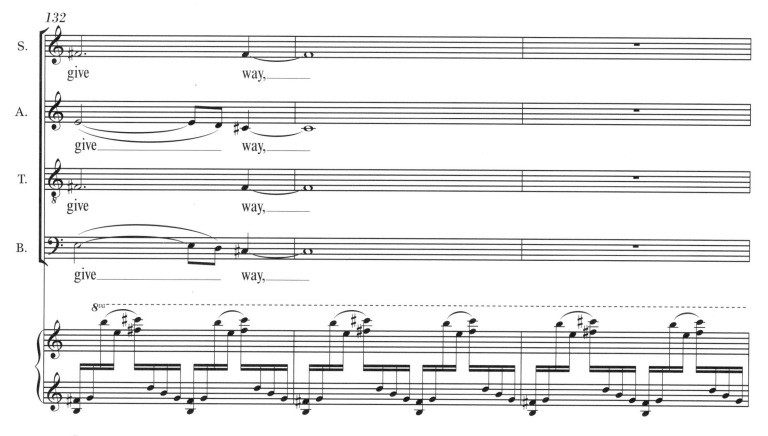

Ped. hold until the end